A CIRCLE OF LOVE

A celebration of Family

ARTWORK BY MONICA STEWART

©1999 Havoc Publishing

ISBN 1-57977-144-0

Published by Havoc Publishing
San Diego, California

Design © 1999 Monica Stewart

Made in China

Please write to us for more information
on Havoc Publishing products.

Havoc Publishing
9808 Waples Street
San Diego, California 92121

THIS BOOK BELONGS TO:

_____

To forget one's ancestors is to be a brook without a source, a tree without a root —PROVERB

CONTENTS

CONTENTS

OUR FAMILY TREE

_____
Great Grandparents
(Father's side)

_____
Great Grandparents

_____
Grandfather

_____
Grandmother

_____
Father

_____
Great Grandparents
(Mother's side)

_____
Great Grandparents

_____
Grandfather

_____
Grandmother

_____
Mother

_____

_____
Children

_____
Aunts

_____
Uncles

_____
Aunts

_____
Uncles

_____

_____
Cousins

The fruit must have a stem before it grows.

- Jabo proverb

ABOUT OUR GREAT GRANDPARENTS
(Father's Father's Family)

Our Great Grandfather's full name is
_____

He was born on this date _____ and he was born in
_____

While growing up, our Great Grandfather lived here
_____

Here are some facts & stories that we remember about our Great Grandfather
_____
_____
_____

Our Great Grandmother's full name is
_____

She was born on this date _____ and she was born in
_____

While growing up, my Great Grandmother lived here
_____
_____

Here are some facts & stories that we remember about our Great Grandmother
_____
_____
_____

The young cannot teach tradition to the old. - Yoruba proverb

ABOUT OUR GREAT GRANDPARENTS

(Father's Mother's Family)

Our Great Grandfather's full name is
_____

He was born on this date _____ and he was born in
_____

While growing up, our Great Grandfather lived here
_____

Here are some facts & stories that we remember about our Great Grandfather
_____
_____
_____

Our Great Grandmother's full name is
_____

She was born on this date _____ and she was born in
_____

While growing up, our Great Grandmother lived here
_____

Here are some facts & stories that we remember about our Great Grandmother
_____
_____
_____

THIS IS OUR GRANDFATHER
(Father's Family)

Our Grandfather's full name is
_____

Some of the nicknames that we call him are
_____

This was the special day he was born _____ and the place he was born
_____

While growing up our Grandfather lived here
_____

Here is a list of some of the schools that our Grandfather attended
_____
_____

Growing up, our Grandfather held jobs working as
_____
_____

Some of our Grandfather's special hobbies and interests are
_____
_____
_____

This is a story that our Grandfather shared with us about a special event that happened to him
_____
_____
_____
_____
_____

THIS IS OUR GRANDMOTHER
(Father's Family)

Our Grandmother's full name is
_____

Some of the nicknames that we call her are
_____

This was the special day she was born _____ and the place she was born
_____

While growing up our Grandmother lived here
_____

Here is a list of some of the schools that our Grandmother attended
_____

_____

Growing up, our Grandmother held jobs working as
_____

_____

Some of our Grandmother's special hobbies and interests are
_____

_____

_____

This is a story that our Grandmother shared with us about a special event that happened to
her
_____

_____

_____

_____

Photograph

Photograph

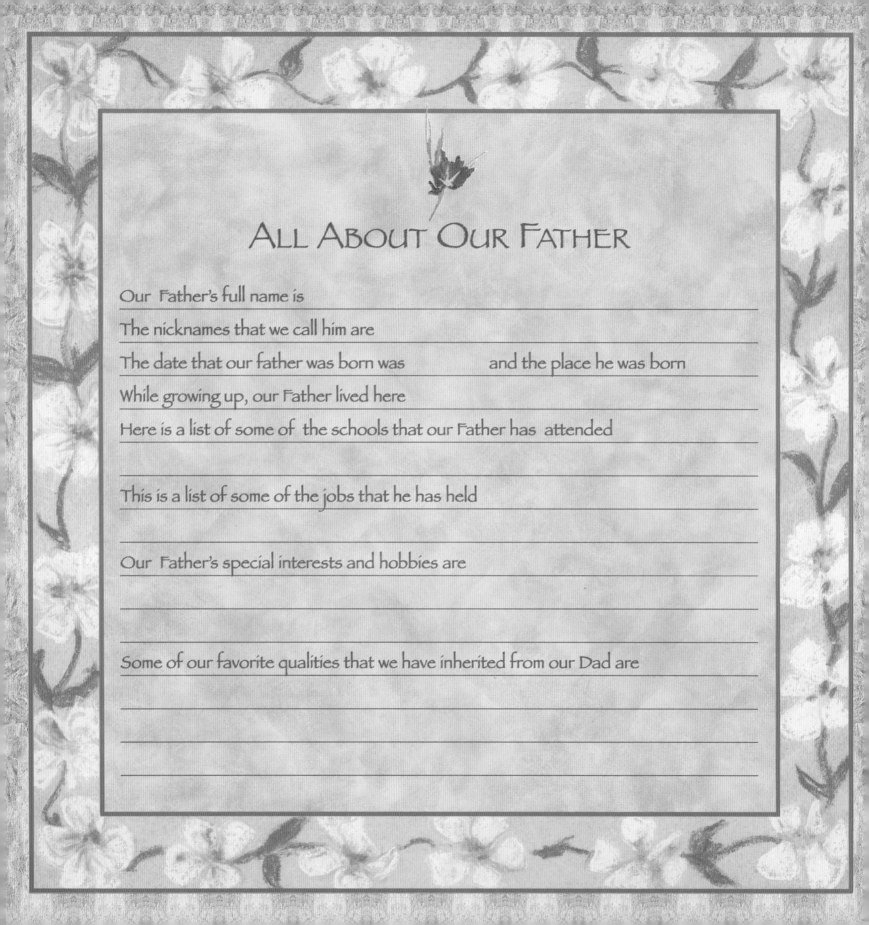

ALL ABOUT OUR FATHER

Our Father's full name is
_____

The nicknames that we call him are
_____

The date that our father was born was _____ and the place he was born _____

While growing up, our Father lived here
_____

Here is a list of some of the schools that our Father has attended
_____
_____

This is a list of some of the jobs that he has held
_____
_____

Our Father's special interests and hobbies are
_____
_____
_____

Some of our favorite qualities that we have inherited from our Dad are
_____
_____
_____
_____

ABOUT OUR AUNTS, UNCLES & COUSINS

(Father's Family)

Here are some stories about times spent with our Aunts, Uncles and our Cousins
_____

_____

_____

_____

_____

_____

_____

_____

_____

_____

About Our Great Grandparents

(Mother's Father's Family)

Our Great Grandfather's full name is
_____

He was born on this date _____ and he was born in _____

While growing up, our Great Grandfather lived here _____

Here are some facts & stories that we remember about our Great Grandfather
_____

_____

Our Great Grandmother's full name is _____

She was born on this date _____ and she was born at _____

While growing up, my Great Grandmother lived here _____

_____

Here are some facts & stories that we remember about our Great Grandmother
_____

_____

_____

_____

ABOUT OUR GREAT GRANDPARENTS

(Mother's Mother's Family)

Our Great Grandfather's full name is
_____

He was born on this date _____ and he was born in _____

While growing up, our Great Grandfather lived here _____

Here are some facts & stories that we remember about our Great Grandfather _____
_____
_____
_____

Our Great Grandmother's full name is
_____

She was born on this date _____ and she was born at _____

While growing up, our Great Grandmother lived here _____
_____

Here are some facts & stories that we remember about our Great Grandmother _____
_____
_____
_____
_____

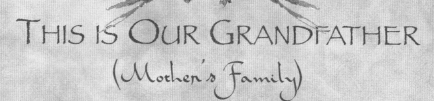

THIS IS OUR GRANDFATHER
(Mother's Family)

Our Grandfather's full name is

Some of the nicknames that we call him are

This was the special day he was born _____ and the place he was born

While growing up our Grandfather lived here

Here is a list of some of the schools that our Grandfather attended

Growing up, our Grandfather held jobs working as

Some of our Grandfather's special hobbies and interests are

This is a story that our Grandfather shared with us about a special event that

happened to him

THIS IS OUR GRANDMOTHER
(Mother's Family)

Our Grandmother's full name is
_____

Some of the nicknames that we call her are
_____

This was the special day she was born _____ and the place she was born _____

While growing up our Grandmother lived here
_____

Here is a list of some of the schools that our Grandmother attended
_____

_____

Growing up, our Grandmother held jobs working as
_____

_____

Some of our Grandmother's special hobbies and interests are
_____

_____

_____

This is a story that our Grandmother shared with us about a special event that

happened to her
_____

_____

THIS IS OUR MOTHER

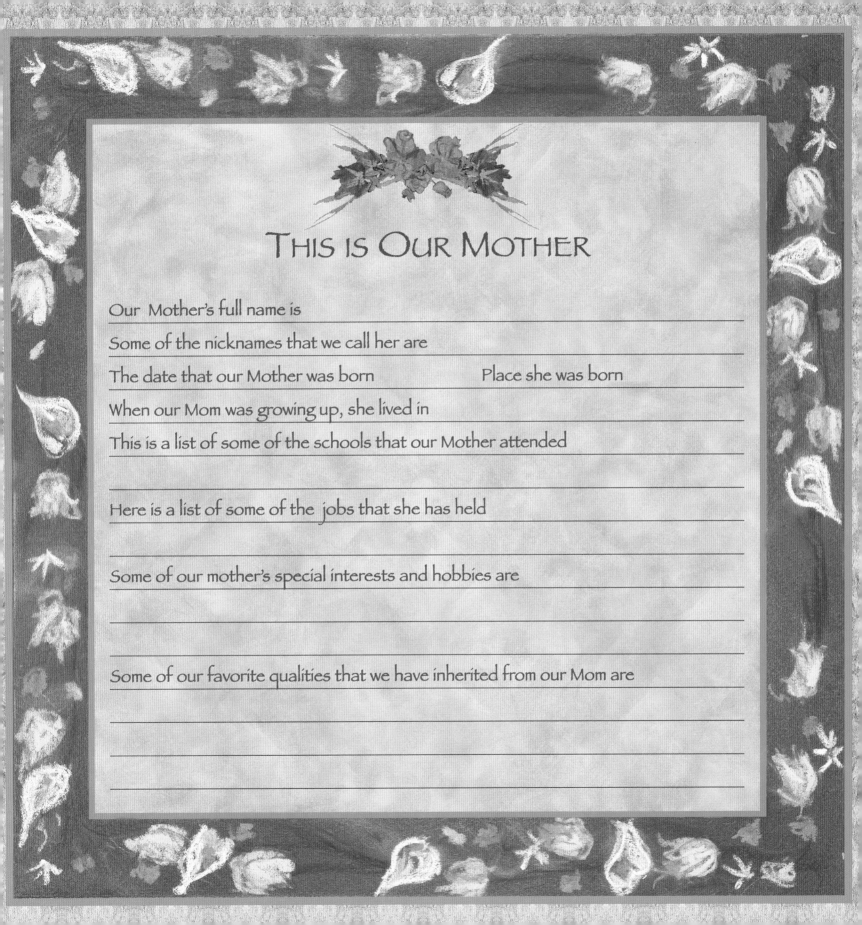

Our Mother's full name is
_____

Some of the nicknames that we call her are
_____

The date that our Mother was born _____   Place she was born _____

When our Mom was growing up, she lived in
_____

This is a list of some of the schools that our Mother attended
_____
_____

Here is a list of some of the jobs that she has held
_____
_____

Some of our mother's special interests and hobbies are
_____
_____
_____

Some of our favorite qualities that we have inherited from our Mom are
_____
_____
_____
_____

ABOUT OUR AUNTS, UNCLES & COUSINS

(Mother's Family)

Here are some stories about times spent with our Aunts, Uncles and our Cousins
_____
_____
_____
_____
_____
_____
_____
_____
_____
_____
_____
_____
_____

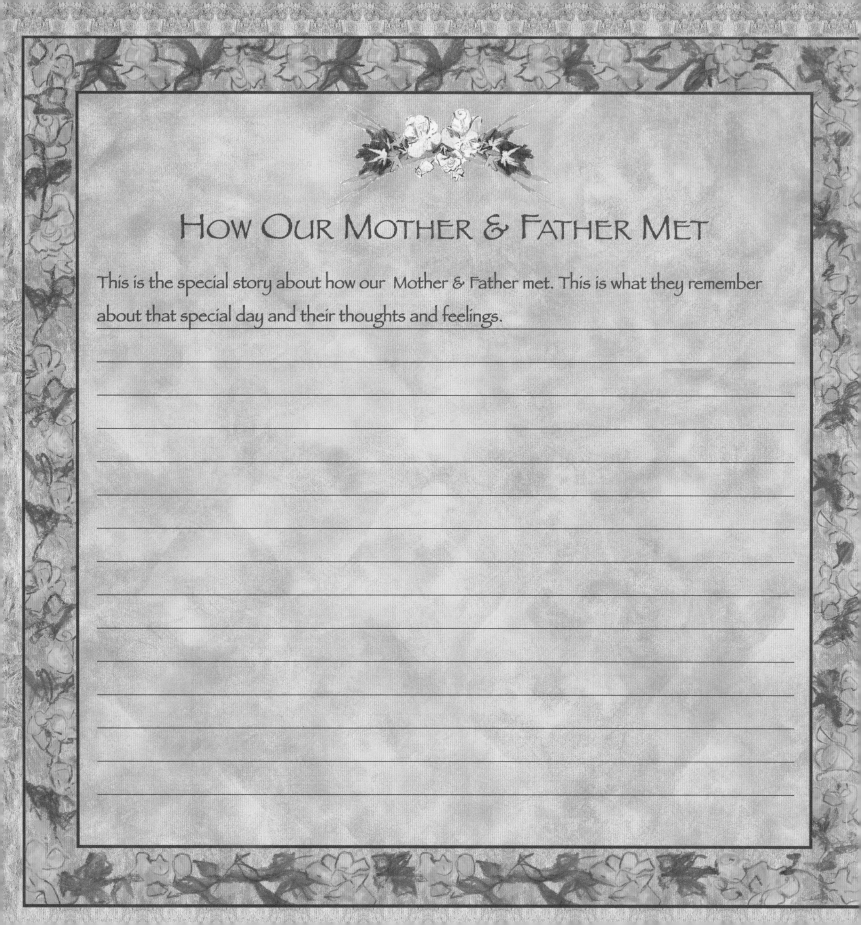

HOW OUR MOTHER & FATHER MET

This is the special story about how our Mother & Father met. This is what they remember about that special day and their thoughts and feelings.

Photograph

Photograph

FAMILY CHILDREN BRING JOY

These are the children in our family

_____

_____

_____

Each and every child is unique and special. This is a little bit about each one of them,

and here are some stories about the fun times that we have spent with them

_____

_____

_____

_____

_____

_____

_____

_____

_____

_____

We do not live for ourselves only, but for our wives and children,
who are as dear to us as those of any other men. - Abraham

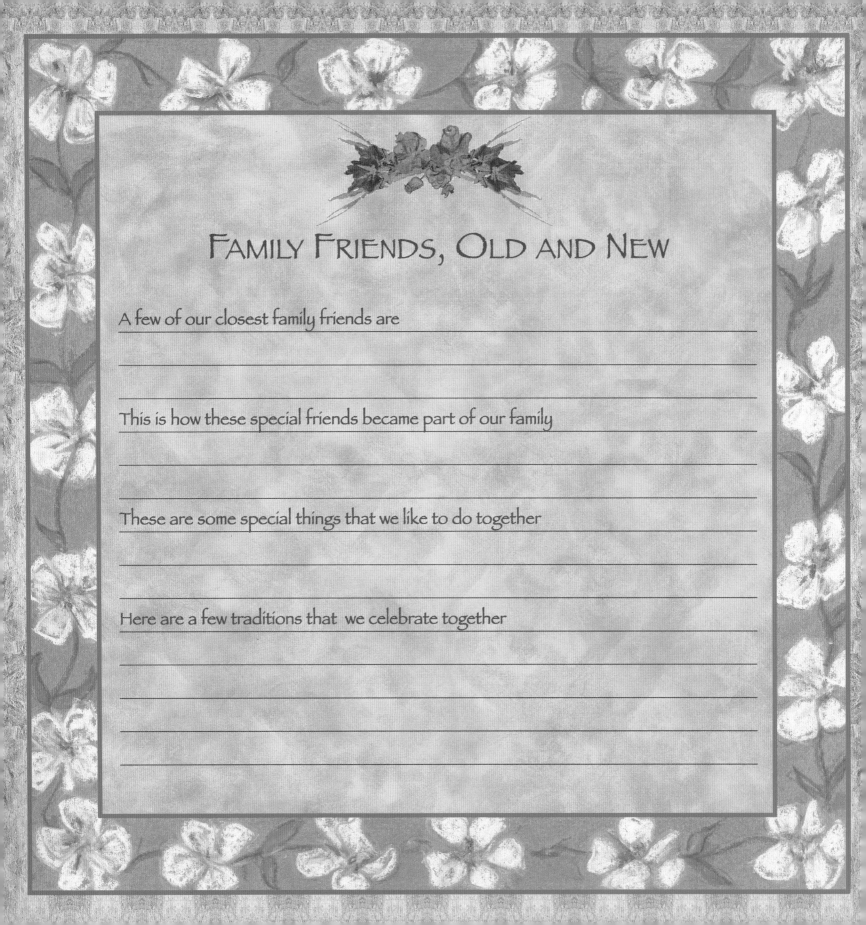

Family Friends, Old and New

A few of our closest family friends are

_____

_____

This is how these special friends became part of our family

_____

_____

These are some special things that we like to do together

_____

_____

Here are a few traditions that we celebrate together

_____

_____

_____

_____

Photograph

Photograph

Springtime Festivities

Some special things that we like to do each and every spring are
_____
_____
_____

The things that we like most about springtime are
_____
_____
_____

Our favorite holidays during the springtime are
_____
_____
_____

A few traditions that we celebrate in the springtime are
_____
_____
_____
_____
_____

WELCOME SUMMER

Special family holidays and celebrations that happen in the summer are

_____

_____

_____

_____

_____

Summer is a time for family and friends and this is what we like to do together

_____

_____

_____

_____

_____

_____

Fall Festivities & Favorites

Our favorite traditions about the fall season are
_____
_____
_____
_____

The favorite fall holidays that our family celebrates are
_____
_____
_____
_____

During the fall season, our family gets together here
_____
_____
_____
_____

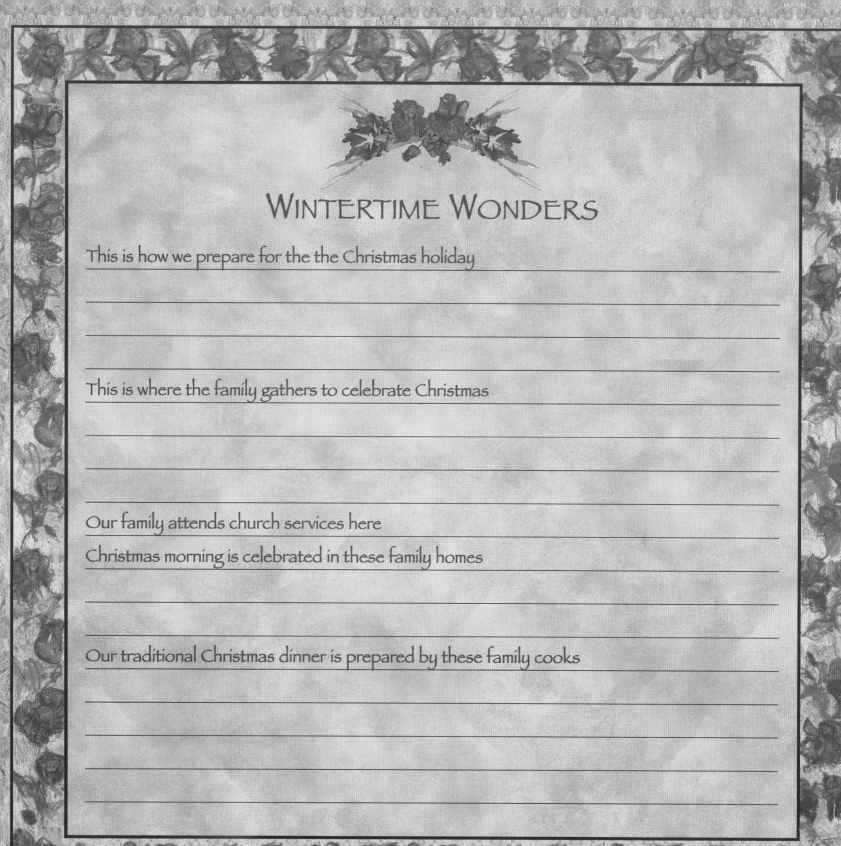

WINTERTIME WONDERS

This is how we prepare for the the Christmas holiday

This is where the family gathers to celebrate Christmas

Our family attends church services here

Christmas morning is celebrated in these family homes

Our traditional Christmas dinner is prepared by these family cooks

Photograph

Photograph

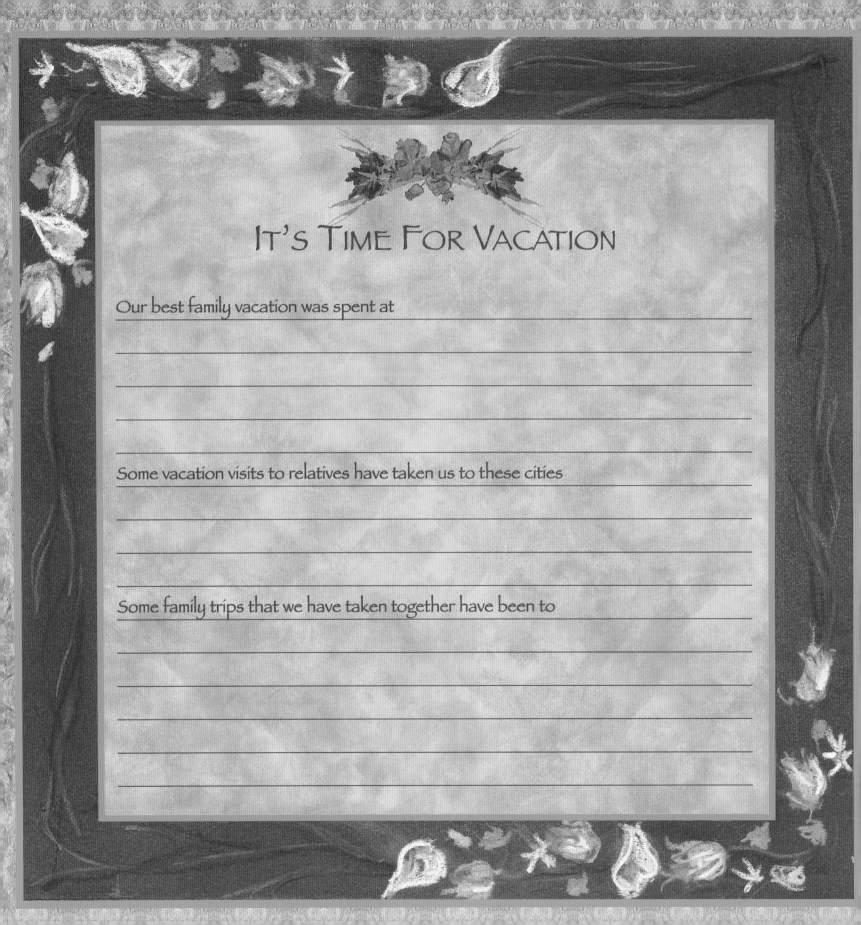

It's Time For Vacation

Our best family vacation was spent at

_____

_____

_____

_____

Some vacation visits to relatives have taken us to these cities

_____

_____

_____

Some family trips that we have taken together have been to

_____

_____

_____

_____

_____

SPECIAL FAMILY TRADITIONS

Here are some of our special family traditions
_____
_____
_____
_____
_____

Every year the women in our family get together to do this
_____
_____
_____

The men in the family get together for this family tradition
_____
_____
_____
_____

HOME SWEET HOME

The address of our family home was

_____

_____

Here is a description of our family home where we grew up

_____

_____

_____

This is a description of our neighborhood

_____

_____

_____

We all lived in this house for this many years

Our favorite neighbors were

_____

_____

_____

As children, our favorite playmates and things to play were

_____

_____

_____

Little by little the bird makes its nest. - Haitian proverb

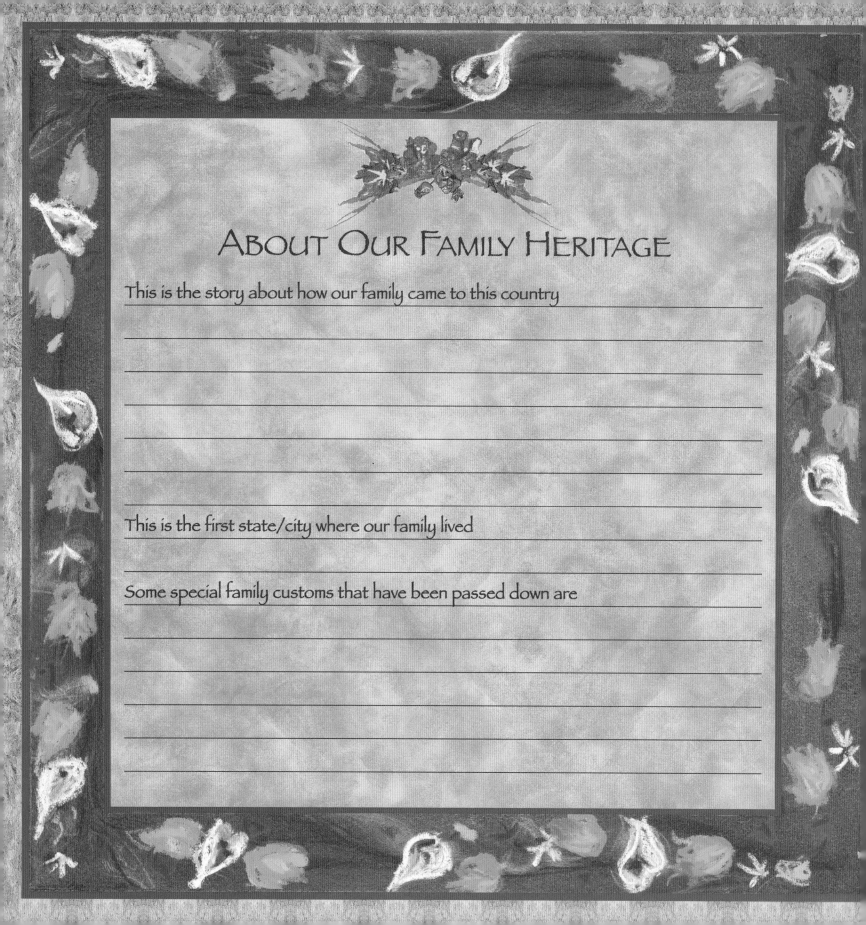

ABOUT OUR FAMILY HERITAGE

This is the story about how our family came to this country

_____

_____

_____

_____

_____

_____

This is the first state/city where our family lived

_____

Some special family customs that have been passed down are

_____

_____

_____

_____

_____

Our family's religious background is

_____

_____

_____

_____

_____

This is where we attend church _____

_____

Our minister's name is _____

Here are somethings that we like to do after church _____

_____

_____

_____

_____

Sticks in a bundle are unbreakable. - Kenyan proverb

Photograph

Photograph

OUR FAMILY FACTS

Our family name means
_____
_____
_____
_____

Our family's origin can be traced backed to
_____
_____
_____
_____
_____
_____

These family members are the most knowledgeable about our family history
_____
_____
_____
_____
_____

A single bracelet does not jingle. - Congo proverb

HAVING SOME FAMILY FUN

Here are some songs that we like to sing
_____
_____
_____
_____

Some lullabies that we grew up with are
_____
_____
_____

Our favorite songs that we sing during the holidays are
_____
_____
_____

The real songbirds in our family are
_____
_____
_____
_____

These family members play instruments
_____
_____

Fun Family Activities

Some movies that we like to watch together are
_____
_____

_____

Here are some books that we've all read, shared and enjoyed
_____
_____

_____

Here are some restaurants that we all like to go to
_____
_____

_____

Some games that the whole family plays
_____
_____

_____

Some family sports that we play together are
_____
_____
_____

_____

photograph

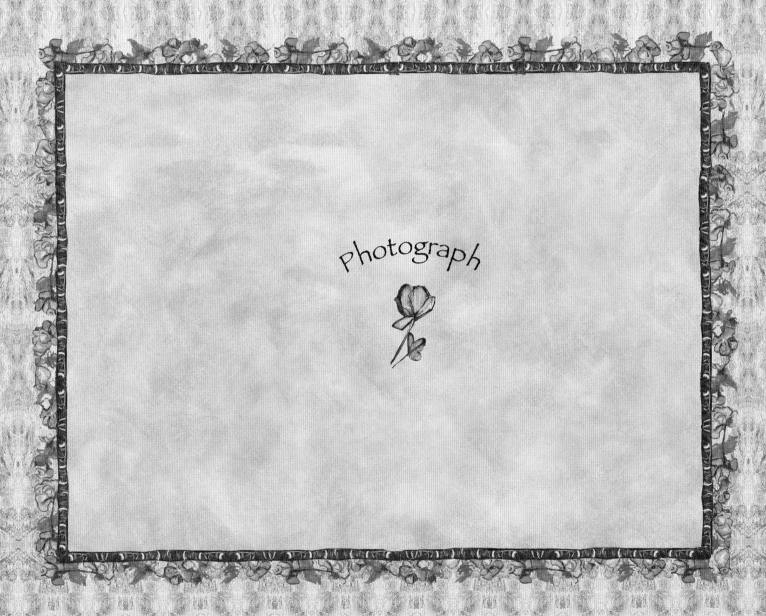

Photograph

FAMILY FOOD

Some favorite family treats are

_____

_____

_____

_____

_____

_____

These are the best cooks in our family

_____

_____

_____

Our favorite food story is about

_____

_____

_____

When hunger gets inside you, nothing else can. – Yoruba proverb

Favorite Recipes

_____   _____

_____   _____

_____   _____

_____   _____

_____   _____

_____   _____

_____   _____

_____   _____

_____   _____

_____   _____

FAMILY IS FOREVER

Here are our thoughts for the future. As we look ahead, we envision this

HAVE YOUR FAMILY AND FRIENDS WRITE
WORDS OF INSPIRATION HERE

Available Record Books from Havoc

A Celebration of Memories
A Circle of Love
Baby
Couples
Family
Forever Friends
Generations
Girlfriends
Grandmother

Grandparents
Heart to Heart
It's All About Me!
Mom
Mothers & Daughters
My Pregnancy
Our Honeymoon
School Days
Sisters
Tying the Knot

Please write to us with your ideas for
additional Havoc Publishing products

Havoc Publishing
9808 Waples Street
San Diego, CA 92121